THE BOOK THAT CHANGED

EVERYTHING

THE BOOK THAT CHANGED
EVERYTHING

Written by Allison Regina Gliot, FSP

Illustrated by Santiago María López Piuma

Pauline
BOOKS & MEDIA

Boston

Library of Congress Control Number: 2023935449

CIP data is available.

ISBN-10: 0-8198-1254-4

ISBN-13: 978-0-8198-1254-4

Illustrated by Santiago María López Piuma

Design by Daughters of St. Paul

"P" and PAULINE are registered trademarks of the Daughters of St. Paul.

Published by Pauline Books & Media, 50 Saint Paul's Avenue, Boston, MA 02130-3491

Printed in Korea

TBTCE SIPSKOGUNKYO3-20 0951254-4

www.pauline.org

Pauline Books & Media is the publishing house of the Daughters of St. Paul, an international congregation of women religious serving the Church with the communications media.

1 2 3 4 5 6 7 8 9   28 27 26 25 24 23

For the Author of my favorite Book

"In the beginning was the Word,
and the Word was with God,
and the Word was God."
— *John 1:1*

Sofia loved reading more than anything.

She spent all her time in a grand old library
that held every book that had ever been written.

Each day, Sofia skipped down the halls
and scampered up the shelves,
exploring the world of words.

From sunrise until sunset, Sofia spent
her time with princesses and penguins,
soldiers and spaceships,
doctors and dinosaurs.

She knew about everything and everyone.

There was just one problem . . .
Nobody knew her.

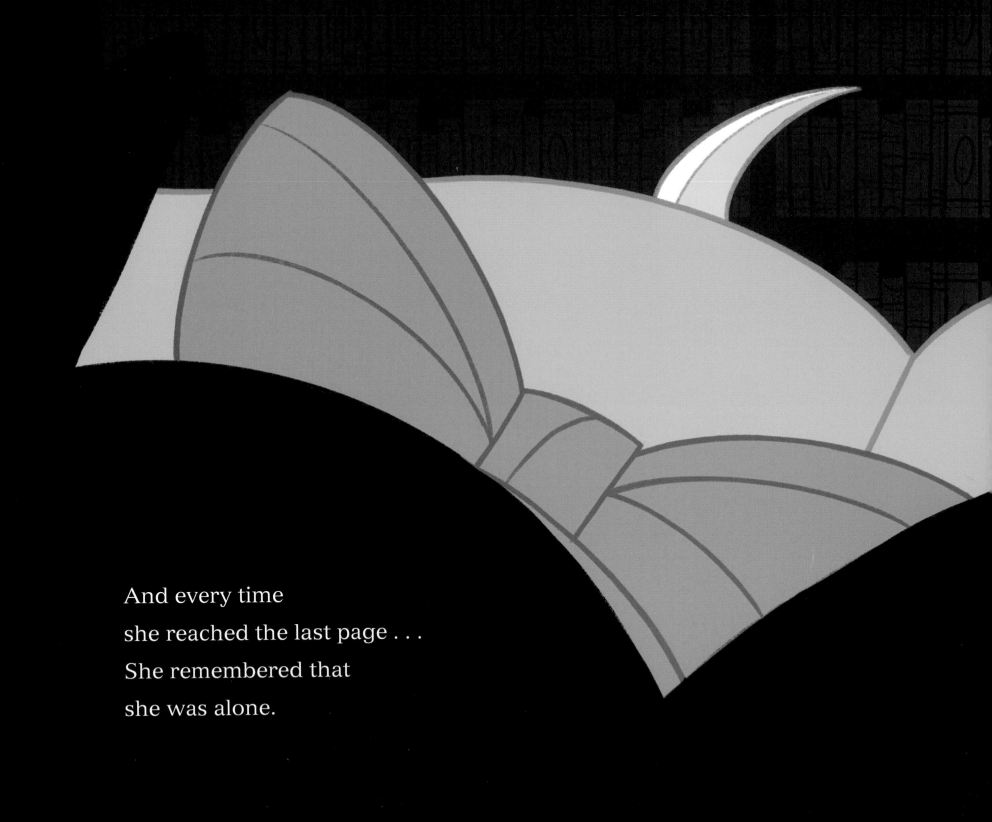

And every time
she reached the last page . . .
She remembered that
she was alone.

Sofia did not know what to do.

She tried to read more stories
to fill the hole inside of her.

But with each happy ending,
she only felt lonelier.

"Something is missing,"
Sofia sighed.

Then one night,
Sofia had a dream.

The next morning, Sofia decided
to search every nook and cranny
of the library.

She did not know exactly
what she was looking for.

But she was certain
she would know
when she found it.

She was right.

There, on the other side of the door, was a Book
like none Sofia had ever seen before.

It felt like a friend calling out to her.
And the words inside . . . were alive!

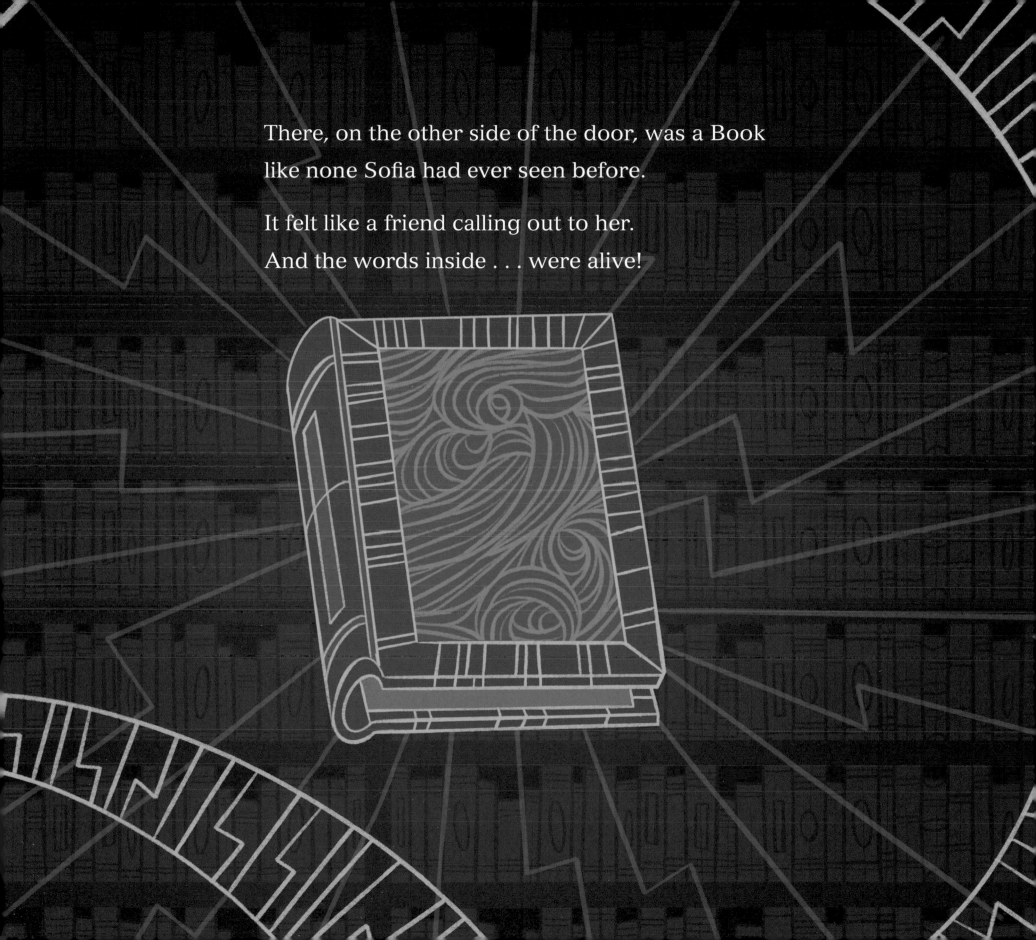

Sofia felt the Book inviting her
to pick it up.

She lifted it like it was made of gold
and carried it to her favorite hideout.

Then she read and read . . .

. . . and read and read,
until finally . . . she fell asleep.

The light she saw in her dream
was the same as the one
that came from the Book.

"Who are you?" she asked.

The voice was kind and gentle, like a warm hug.

"I am the Word of God. My name is Jesus."

Sofia gasped. "Jesus? I read about you in the Book!"

"You were not *just* reading about me, Sofia.
I was speaking to you."

"That Book is my voice.
Whenever you read it, we are together."

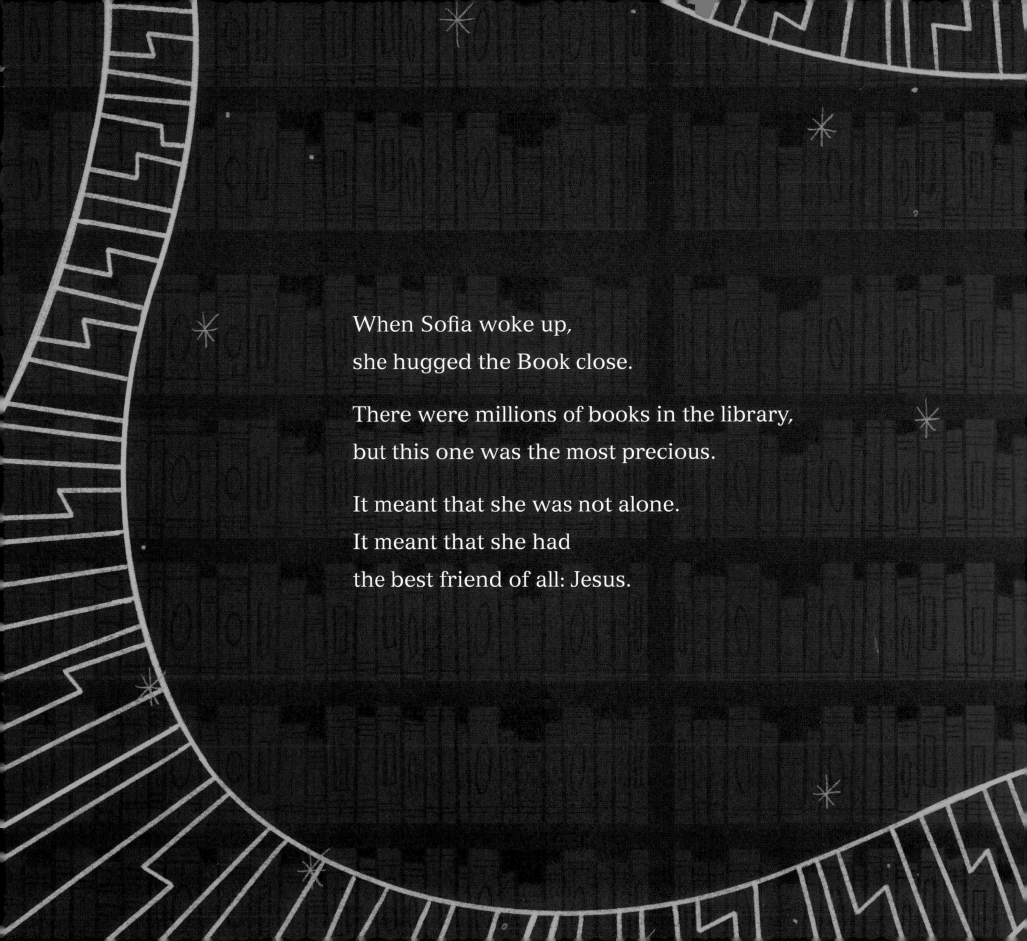

When Sofia woke up,
she hugged the Book close.

There were millions of books in the library,
but this one was the most precious.

It meant that she was not alone.
It meant that she had
the best friend of all: Jesus.

Sofia spent time with her friend every day.

She learned what made him laugh
and she learned what made him cry.

She learned about his mission
and she learned about his promises.

But most of all, she learned
about his love.

Even when she read every page,
the Book was never over.

Jesus always had something new
to say to her.

"Do you like my Book, Sofia?"

"Yes, more than anything!"
Sofia's heart had never felt so full.

"Would you like to hear the rest
of the story?"

Sofia's eyes widened. "There's more?"

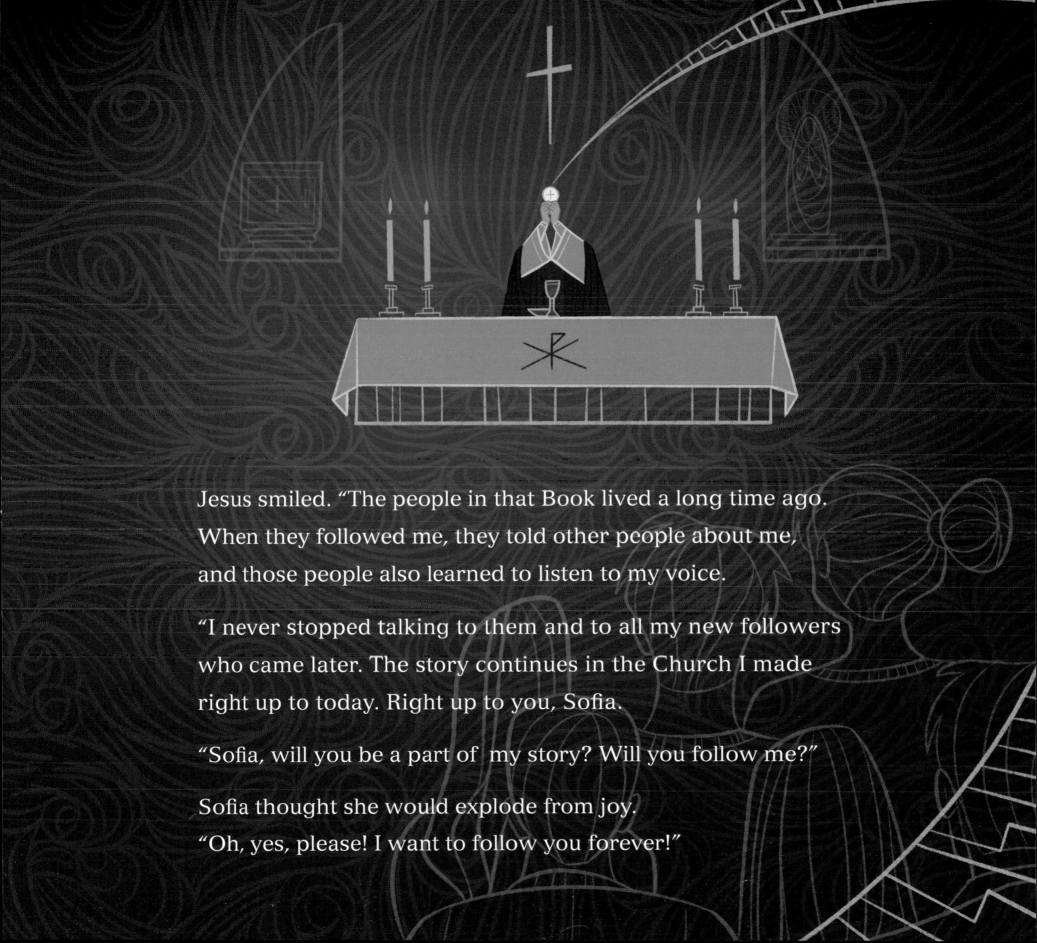

Jesus smiled. "The people in that Book lived a long time ago.
When they followed me, they told other people about me,
and those people also learned to listen to my voice.

"I never stopped talking to them and to all my new followers
who came later. The story continues in the Church I made
right up to today. Right up to you, Sofia.

"Sofia, will you be a part of my story? Will you follow me?"

Sofia thought she would explode from joy.
"Oh, yes, please! I want to follow you forever!"

"Then come, my little one.
Do not be afraid. I am with you.
I have so much to show you."

About the Author

Sister Allison Regina Gliot, FSP, has never lived in a library, although she has often wanted to. She loves writing stories for children and teens, spending time with the sisters in her community (the Daughters of Saint Paul), and being with her best friend: Jesus.

About the Illustrator

Santi, known as Samlo in the entertainment industry, is an Argentinian creative who tries to follow God's will in his life and work. After attending the architectural school at the University of Buenos Aires, he decided to change the course of his life by pursuing his childhood passion of drawing—embarking on a creative professional career. It's a joy to put yourself at the service of others and to help others to grow closer to heaven through art and creativity.

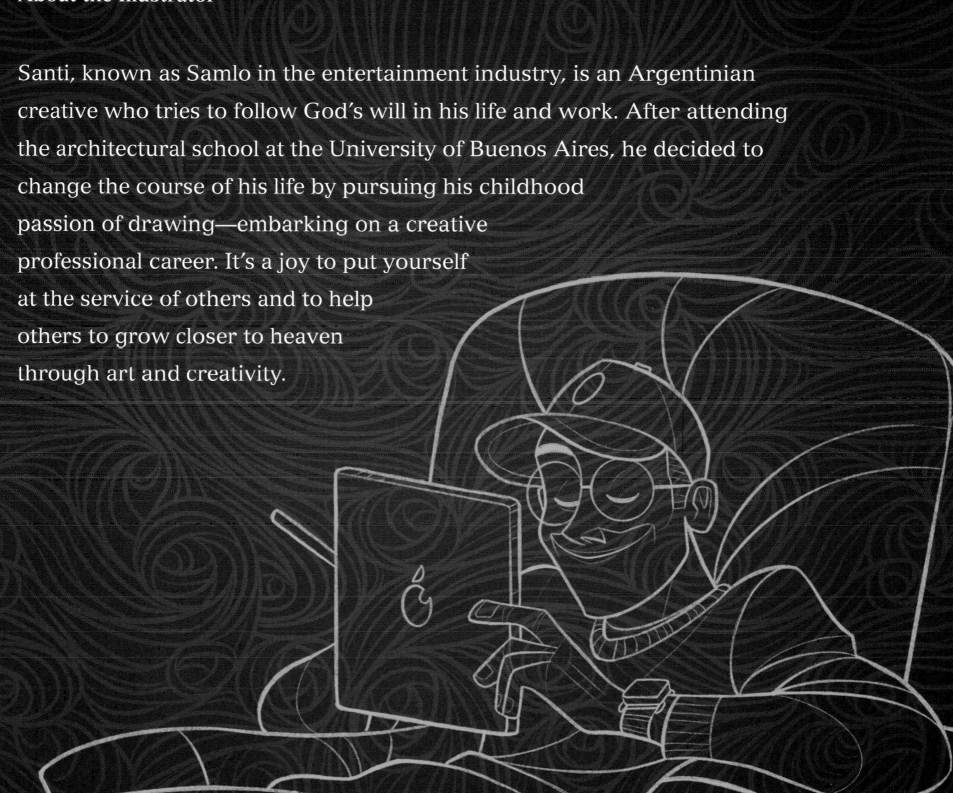

Who are the Daughters of St. Paul?

We are Catholic sisters with a mission. Our task is to bring the love of Jesus to everyone like Saint Paul did. You can find us in over 50 countries. Our founder, Blessed James Alberione, showed us how to reach out to the world through the media. That's why we publish books, make movies and apps, record music, broadcast on radio, perform concerts, help people at our bookstores, visit parishes, use social media and the Internet, and pray for all of you.